50 STATES
Travel Journal

If found, please return to

ABOUT ME

NAME

DATE OF BIRTH

NATIONALITY

COUNTRY OF RESIDENCE

NOTES

MY FAVORITE MEMORY FROM PAST TRAVELS IS

I LOVE TO TRAVEL BECAUSE

MY FAVORITE PLACE TO VISIT IS

MY PREFERRED KIND OF TRIP IS

IF I COULD BE ANYWHERE, I'D CHOOSE

I BOUGHT/RECEIVED THIS TRAVEL JOURNAL BECAUSE

ON THE MAP

WASHINGTON
MONTANA
NORTH DAKOT
ALASKA
PACIFIC OCEAN
OREGON
IDAHO
SOUTH DAKOT
WYOMING
NEBRAS
NEVADA
UTAH
COLORADO
CALIFORNIA
ARIZONA
NEW MEXICO
PACIFIC OCEAN
PACIFIC OCEAN
HAWAII

NEW
HAMPSHIRE
MINNESOTA
VERMONT
MAINE
WISCONSIN
MICHIGAN
NEW YORK
MASSACHUSETTS
IOWA
RHODE
ISLAND
PENNSYLVANIA
ILLINOIS
INDIANA
OHIO
NEW
JERSEY
CONNECTICUT
WEST
VIRGINIA
KANSAS
MISSOURI
DELAWARE
KENTUCKY
MARYLAND
VIRGINIA
TENNESSEE
OKLAHOMA
NORTH
CAROLINA
ARKANSAS
SOUTH
CAROLINA
MISSISSIPPI
ALABAMA
GEORGIA
TEXAS
ATLANTIC
OCEAN
LOUISIANA
FLORIDA
N

ALABAMA

WHEN I'M GOING

WHO I'M GOING WITH

WHERE I'M STAYING

REASON FOR GOING

PLACES I WANT TO VISIT

EXPERIENCES I WANT TO HAVE

ALASKA

WHEN I'M GOING

WHO I'M GOING WITH

WHERE I'M STAYING

REASON FOR GOING

PLACES I WANT TO VISIT

EXPERIENCES I WANT TO HAVE

ARIZONA

WHEN I'M GOING

WHO I'M GOING WITH

WHERE I'M STAYING

REASON FOR GOING

PLACES I WANT TO VISIT

- ○
- ○
- ○
- ○
- ○

EXPERIENCES I WANT TO HAVE

- ○
- ○
- ○
- ○
- ○

ARKANSAS

WHEN I'M GOING

WHO I'M GOING WITH

WHERE I'M STAYING

REASON FOR GOING

PLACES I WANT TO VISIT

- ○
- ○
- ○
- ○
- ○

EXPERIENCES I WANT TO HAVE

- ○
- ○
- ○
- ○
- ○

CALIFORNIA

WHEN I'M GOING

WHO I'M GOING WITH

WHERE I'M STAYING

REASON FOR GOING

PLACES I WANT TO VISIT

- ○
- ○
- ○
- ○
- ○

EXPERIENCES I WANT TO HAVE

- ○
- ○
- ○
- ○
- ○

COLORADO

WHEN I'M GOING

WHO I'M GOING WITH

WHERE I'M STAYING

REASON FOR GOING

PLACES I WANT TO VISIT

- [ ]
- [ ]
- [ ]
- [ ]
- [ ]

EXPERIENCES I WANT TO HAVE

- [ ]
- [ ]
- [ ]
- [ ]
- [ ]

CONNECTICUT

WHEN I'M GOING

WHO I'M GOING WITH

WHERE I'M STAYING

REASON FOR GOING

PLACES I WANT TO VISIT

- ○
- ○
- ○
- ○
- ○

EXPERIENCES I WANT TO HAVE

- ○
- ○
- ○
- ○
- ○

DELAWARE

WHEN I'M GOING

WHO I'M GOING WITH

WHERE I'M STAYING

REASON FOR GOING

PLACES I WANT TO VISIT

- ○
- ○
- ○
- ○
- ○

EXPERIENCES I WANT TO HAVE

- ○
- ○
- ○
- ○
- ○

FLORIDA

WHEN I'M GOING

WHO I'M GOING WITH

WHERE I'M STAYING

REASON FOR GOING

PLACES I WANT TO VISIT

EXPERIENCES I WANT TO HAVE

GEORGIA

WHEN I'M GOING

WHO I'M GOING WITH

WHERE I'M STAYING

REASON FOR GOING

PLACES I WANT TO VISIT

- ○
- ○
- ○
- ○
- ○

EXPERIENCES I WANT TO HAVE

- ○
- ○
- ○
- ○
- ○

HAWAII

WHEN I'M GOING

WHO I'M GOING WITH

WHERE I'M STAYING

REASON FOR GOING

PLACES I WANT TO VISIT

- ○
- ○
- ○
- ○
- ○

EXPERIENCES I WANT TO HAVE

- ○
- ○
- ○
- ○
- ○

IDAHO

WHEN I'M GOING

WHO I'M GOING WITH

WHERE I'M STAYING

REASON FOR GOING

PLACES I WANT TO VISIT

- ○
- ○
- ○
- ○
- ○

EXPERIENCES I WANT TO HAVE

- ○
- ○
- ○
- ○
- ○

ILLINOIS

WHEN I'M GOING

WHO I'M GOING WITH

WHERE I'M STAYING

REASON FOR GOING

PLACES I WANT TO VISIT

- ○
- ○
- ○
- ○
- ○

EXPERIENCES I WANT TO HAVE

- ○
- ○
- ○
- ○
- ○

INDIANA

WHEN I'M GOING

WHO I'M GOING WITH

WHERE I'M STAYING

REASON FOR GOING

PLACES I WANT TO VISIT

EXPERIENCES I WANT TO HAVE

IOWA

WHEN I'M GOING

WHO I'M GOING WITH

WHERE I'M STAYING

REASON FOR GOING

PLACES I WANT TO VISIT

EXPERIENCES I WANT TO HAVE

KANSAS

WHEN I'M GOING

WHO I'M GOING WITH

WHERE I'M STAYING

REASON FOR GOING

PLACES I WANT TO VISIT

- ○
- ○
- ○
- ○
- ○

EXPERIENCES I WANT TO HAVE

- ○
- ○
- ○
- ○
- ○

KENTUCKY

WHEN I'M GOING

WHO I'M GOING WITH

WHERE I'M STAYING

REASON FOR GOING

PLACES I WANT TO VISIT

- ○
- ○
- ○
- ○
- ○

EXPERIENCES I WANT TO HAVE

- ○
- ○
- ○
- ○
- ○

LOUISIANA

WHEN I'M GOING

WHO I'M GOING WITH

WHERE I'M STAYING

REASON FOR GOING

PLACES I WANT TO VISIT

- ○
- ○
- ○
- ○
- ○

EXPERIENCES I WANT TO HAVE

- ○
- ○
- ○
- ○
- ○

MAINE

WHEN I'M GOING

WHO I'M GOING WITH

WHERE I'M STAYING

REASON FOR GOING

PLACES I WANT TO VISIT

- ○
- ○
- ○
- ○
- ○

EXPERIENCES I WANT TO HAVE

- ○
- ○
- ○
- ○
- ○

MARYLAND

WHEN I'M GOING

WHO I'M GOING WITH

WHERE I'M STAYING

REASON FOR GOING

PLACES I WANT TO VISIT

EXPERIENCES I WANT TO HAVE

MASSACHUSETTS

WHEN I'M GOING

WHO I'M GOING WITH

WHERE I'M STAYING

REASON FOR GOING

PLACES I WANT TO VISIT

- ○
- ○
- ○
- ○
- ○

EXPERIENCES I WANT TO HAVE

- ○
- ○
- ○
- ○
- ○

MICHIGAN

WHEN I'M GOING

WHO I'M GOING WITH

WHERE I'M STAYING

REASON FOR GOING

PLACES I WANT TO VISIT

- ○
- ○
- ○
- ○
- ○

EXPERIENCES I WANT TO HAVE

- ○
- ○
- ○
- ○
- ○

MINNESOTA

WHEN I'M GOING

WHO I'M GOING WITH

WHERE I'M STAYING

REASON FOR GOING

PLACES I WANT TO VISIT

- ○
- ○
- ○
- ○
- ○

EXPERIENCES I WANT TO HAVE

- ○
- ○
- ○
- ○
- ○

MISSISSIPPI

WHEN I'M GOING

WHO I'M GOING WITH

WHERE I'M STAYING

REASON FOR GOING

PLACES I WANT TO VISIT

- ○
- ○
- ○
- ○
- ○

EXPERIENCES I WANT TO HAVE

- ○
- ○
- ○
- ○
- ○

MISSOURI

WHEN I'M GOING

WHO I'M GOING WITH

WHERE I'M STAYING

REASON FOR GOING

PLACES I WANT TO VISIT

EXPERIENCES I WANT TO HAVE

MONTANA

WHEN I'M GOING

WHO I'M GOING WITH

WHERE I'M STAYING

REASON FOR GOING

PLACES I WANT TO VISIT

- ○
- ○
- ○
- ○
- ○

EXPERIENCES I WANT TO HAVE

- ○
- ○
- ○
- ○
- ○

NEBRASKA

WHEN I'M GOING

WHO I'M GOING WITH

WHERE I'M STAYING

REASON FOR GOING

PLACES I WANT TO VISIT

EXPERIENCES I WANT TO HAVE

NEVADA

WHEN I'M GOING

WHO I'M GOING WITH

WHERE I'M STAYING

REASON FOR GOING

PLACES I WANT TO VISIT

EXPERIENCES I WANT TO HAVE

NEW HAMPSHIRE

WHEN I'M GOING

WHO I'M GOING WITH

WHERE I'M STAYING

REASON FOR GOING

PLACES I WANT TO VISIT

- ○
- ○
- ○
- ○
- ○

EXPERIENCES I WANT TO HAVE

- ○
- ○
- ○
- ○
- ○

NEW JERSEY

WHEN I'M GOING

WHO I'M GOING WITH

WHERE I'M STAYING

REASON FOR GOING

PLACES I WANT TO VISIT

- ○
- ○
- ○
- ○
- ○

EXPERIENCES I WANT TO HAVE

- ○
- ○
- ○
- ○
- ○

NEW MEXICO

WHEN I'M GOING

WHO I'M GOING WITH

WHERE I'M STAYING

REASON FOR GOING

PLACES I WANT TO VISIT

- ○
- ○
- ○
- ○
- ○

EXPERIENCES I WANT TO HAVE

- ○
- ○
- ○
- ○
- ○

NEW YORK

WHEN I'M GOING

WHO I'M GOING WITH

WHERE I'M STAYING

REASON FOR GOING

PLACES I WANT TO VISIT

EXPERIENCES I WANT TO HAVE

NORTH CAROLINA

WHEN I'M GOING

WHO I'M GOING WITH

WHERE I'M STAYING

REASON FOR GOING

PLACES I WANT TO VISIT

EXPERIENCES I WANT TO HAVE

NORTH DAKOTA

WHEN I'M GOING

WHO I'M GOING WITH

WHERE I'M STAYING

REASON FOR GOING

PLACES I WANT TO VISIT

EXPERIENCES I WANT TO HAVE

OHIO

WHEN I'M GOING

WHO I'M GOING WITH

WHERE I'M STAYING

REASON FOR GOING

PLACES I WANT TO VISIT

- ○
- ○
- ○
- ○
- ○

EXPERIENCES I WANT TO HAVE

- ○
- ○
- ○
- ○
- ○

OKLAHOMA

WHEN I'M GOING

WHO I'M GOING WITH

WHERE I'M STAYING

REASON FOR GOING

PLACES I WANT TO VISIT

- ○
- ○
- ○
- ○
- ○

EXPERIENCES I WANT TO HAVE

- ○
- ○
- ○
- ○
- ○

OREGON

WHEN I'M GOING

WHO I'M GOING WITH

WHERE I'M STAYING

REASON FOR GOING

PLACES I WANT TO VISIT

EXPERIENCES I WANT TO HAVE

PENNSYLVANIA

WHEN I'M GOING

WHO I'M GOING WITH

WHERE I'M STAYING

REASON FOR GOING

PLACES I WANT TO VISIT

- ○
- ○
- ○
- ○
- ○

EXPERIENCES I WANT TO HAVE

- ○
- ○
- ○
- ○
- ○

RHODE ISLAND

WHEN I'M GOING

WHO I'M GOING WITH

WHERE I'M STAYING

REASON FOR GOING

PLACES I WANT TO VISIT

EXPERIENCES I WANT TO HAVE

SOUTH CAROLINA

WHEN I'M GOING

WHO I'M GOING WITH

WHERE I'M STAYING

REASON FOR GOING

PLACES I WANT TO VISIT

- ○
- ○
- ○
- ○
- ○

EXPERIENCES I WANT TO HAVE

- ○
- ○
- ○
- ○
- ○

SOUTH DAKOTA

WHEN I'M GOING

WHO I'M GOING WITH

WHERE I'M STAYING

REASON FOR GOING

PLACES I WANT TO VISIT

- ○
- ○
- ○
- ○
- ○

EXPERIENCES I WANT TO HAVE

- ○
- ○
- ○
- ○
- ○

TENNESSEE

WHEN I'M GOING

WHO I'M GOING WITH

WHERE I'M STAYING

REASON FOR GOING

PLACES I WANT TO VISIT

- ○
- ○
- ○
- ○
- ○

EXPERIENCES I WANT TO HAVE

- ○
- ○
- ○
- ○
- ○

TEXAS

WHEN I'M GOING

WHO I'M GOING WITH

WHERE I'M STAYING

REASON FOR GOING

PLACES I WANT TO VISIT

EXPERIENCES I WANT TO HAVE

UTAH

WHEN I'M GOING

WHO I'M GOING WITH

WHERE I'M STAYING

REASON FOR GOING

PLACES I WANT TO VISIT

- ○
- ○
- ○
- ○
- ○

EXPERIENCES I WANT TO HAVE

- ○
- ○
- ○
- ○
- ○

VERMONT

WHEN I'M GOING

WHO I'M GOING WITH

WHERE I'M STAYING

REASON FOR GOING

PLACES I WANT TO VISIT

- ○
- ○
- ○
- ○
- ○

EXPERIENCES I WANT TO HAVE

- ○
- ○
- ○
- ○
- ○

VIRGINIA

WHEN I'M GOING

WHO I'M GOING WITH

WHERE I'M STAYING

REASON FOR GOING

PLACES I WANT TO VISIT

EXPERIENCES I WANT TO HAVE

WASHINGTON

WHEN I'M GOING

WHO I'M GOING WITH

WHERE I'M STAYING

REASON FOR GOING

PLACES I WANT TO VISIT

- ○
- ○
- ○
- ○
- ○

EXPERIENCES I WANT TO HAVE

- ○
- ○
- ○
- ○
- ○

WEST VIRGINIA

WHEN I'M GOING

WHO I'M GOING WITH

WHERE I'M STAYING

REASON FOR GOING

PLACES I WANT TO VISIT

- ○
- ○
- ○
- ○
- ○

EXPERIENCES I WANT TO HAVE

- ○
- ○
- ○
- ○
- ○

WISCONSIN

WHEN I'M GOING

WHO I'M GOING WITH

WHERE I'M STAYING

REASON FOR GOING

PLACES I WANT TO VISIT

EXPERIENCES I WANT TO HAVE

WYOMING

WHEN I'M GOING

WHO I'M GOING WITH

WHERE I'M STAYING

REASON FOR GOING

PLACES I WANT TO VISIT

- ○
- ○
- ○
- ○
- ○

EXPERIENCES I WANT TO HAVE

- ○
- ○
- ○
- ○
- ○

NOTES

DK | Penguin Random House

Published in Great Britain by Dorling Kindersley Limited, 20 Vauxhall Bridge Road, London SW1V 2SA

Published in the United States by DK Publishing, a division of Penguin Random House LLC, 1745 Broadway, 20th Floor, New York, NY 10019

10 9 8 7 6 5 4 3 2
002-357985-Apr/2026

Jacket Illustrations David Sierra Martínez

ISBN: 978 0 2418 1602 8

Printed and bound in China.
www.dk.com

MIX
Paper | Supporting responsible forestry
FSC™ C018179
FSC www.fsc.org

This book was made with Forest Stewardship Council™ certified paper – one small step in DK's commitment to a sustainable future.
Learn more at **www.dk.com/uk/information/sustainability**

ALABAMA

ALASKA

ARIZONA

ARKANSAS

California

Colorado

Connecticut

Delaware

FLORIDA

GEORGIA

Hawaii

IDAHO

Illinois

Indiana

IOWA

KANSAS

KENTUCKY

Louisiana

MAINE

Maryland

MASSACHUSETTS

MICHIGAN

MINNESOTA

MISSISSIPPI

MISSOURI

MONTANA

NEBRASKA

NEVADA

NEW
HAMPSHIRE

New
JERSEY

NEW MEXICO

NEW YORK

North
CAROLINA

North
DAKOTA

OHIO

OKLAHOMA

Oregon

PENNSYLVANIA

RHODE
Island

SOUTH CAROLINA

South
DAKOTA

TENNESSEE

TEXAS

UTAH

VERMONT

VIRGINIA

WASHINGTON

west
VIRGINIA

Wisconsin

WYOMING